SMART INVESTING MADE EASY

A Beginner's Guide to Building a Portfolio

Charles Chanthunya

TABLE OF CONTENTS

CHAPTER ONE

INTRODUCTION

Investing can seem intimidating and overwhelming, especially for beginners. With so many investment options, conflicting advice, and the fear of losing money, it's easy to understand why many people shy away from investing altogether. However, investing doesn't have to be difficult or frightening. In fact, it can be an incredibly powerful tool for building wealth and achieving your financial goals.

This book is designed to help you navigate the world of investing and provide you with the knowledge and tools you need to build a successful portfolio. Whether you're new to investing or have some experience but want to deepen your knowledge, this book is for you.

We'll start by covering the basics of investing, including the different types of investments and how the stock market works. Then, we'll move on to getting started, helping you set investment goals, assess your risk tolerance, and create a budget. From there, we'll dive into building a portfolio, covering topics like asset allocation, diversification, and choosing the right investments. We'll also cover different investment strategies, such as value investing and growth investing, and provide tips for successful investing.

Finally, we'll discuss retirement planning and how investing can help you achieve your retirement goals. By the end of this book, you'll have a solid understanding of how to build a successful investment portfolio and the confidence to start investing on your own. So, let's get started on your journey to smart investing!

Explanation of investing and portfolio building

The act of investing involves putting money into something with the hope of earning a return on it in the future. Investing can take many forms, such as buying stocks, bonds, mutual funds, real estate, or even starting your own business. The goal of investing is to grow your wealth over time by earning a return on your investment.

One way to invest is by building a portfolio, which is simply a collection of different investments that are chosen and managed to achieve specific financial goals. The purpose of building a portfolio is to spread your investments across different asset classes, such as stocks, bonds, and cash, in order to reduce the overall risk of your investment.

The foundation of portfolio building is asset allocation, which is the process of deciding how much of your portfolio should be invested in each asset class. The key is to find the right balance of investments that will help you achieve your goals while minimizing risk.

There are different ways to approach asset allocation, and the right strategy depends on factors such as your risk tolerance, investment goals, and time horizon. A common rule of thumb is to invest a percentage of your portfolio in stocks based on your age. For example, if you're 30 years old, you might invest 70% of your portfolio in stocks and the rest in bonds and cash. As you get older, you might gradually shift your investments to a more conservative mix.

Stocks are often considered riskier investments because their prices can be volatile and can fluctuate based on market conditions. However, they also offer the potential for higher returns over the long-term. Bonds, on the other hand, are generally considered less risky because they offer a fixed rate of return and are less affected by market fluctuations.

It's important to note that there is no one-size-fits-all approach to investing, and what works for one person may not work for another. The key is to find the right balance of investments that aligns with your investment goals, risk tolerance, and time horizon.

Diversification is also an important component of portfolio building. Diversification means spreading your investments across different asset classes, sectors, and industries to reduce risk. You can lessen the effect of any one investment on your whole portfolio by diversifying your holdings.

For example, if you only invest in technology stocks and the technology sector experiences a downturn, your entire portfolio could suffer. But if you diversify your investments across different sectors, such as healthcare, consumer goods, and finance, you can reduce the impact of any one sector on your portfolio.

Another important aspect of portfolio building is choosing the right investments. There are many different types of investments to choose from, including individual stocks, bonds, mutual funds, and exchange-traded funds (ETFs).

Individual stocks are shares of a company that are traded on the stock market. When you buy a stock, you own a piece of the company and have a share in its profits and losses. Buying individual stocks can be risky, as the success of the stock depends on the success of the company. However, buying individual stocks can also be rewarding, as successful companies can offer significant returns.

Bonds, on the other hand, are corporate or governmental debt securities. When you buy a bond, you're essentially lending money to the issuer and receiving interest payments in return. Although they provide smaller returns than stocks, bonds are typically thought to be less hazardous.

Mutual funds are a sort of investment where money is pooled from numerous individuals and used to purchase a diverse portfolio of stocks, bonds, or other securities. You can acquire exposure to a variety of investments by investing in a mutual fund rather than picking and managing individual investments yourself. Mutual funds are often managed by professional investment managers who make decisions on behalf of the fund's investors.

ETFs are similar to mutual funds in that they offer investors a diversified portfolio of investments. However, ETFs are traded on the stock market like individual stocks, making them more flexible and allowing investors to buy and sell shares throughout the trading day.

Choosing the right investments for your portfolio depends on your investment goals, risk tolerance, and time horizon. It's important to do your research and consider factors such as the historical performance of the investment, the fees associated with the investment, and the overall risk level of the investment.

Value investing and growth investing are two common investment strategies that can be used to choose individual stocks or mutual funds. Value investing involves looking for stocks that are undervalued by the market, with the expectation that the stock's price will eventually rise to reflect its true value. Growth investing, on the other hand, involves looking for stocks of companies that are expected to experience above-average growth in earnings or revenue.

It's important to note that there is no one "right" investment strategy, and what works for one investor may not work for another. The key is to find an investment strategy that aligns with your investment goals, risk tolerance, and time horizon.

In summary, investing can be a powerful tool for building wealth over time. Building a portfolio involves asset allocation, diversification, and choosing the right investments. By spreading your investments across different asset classes and industries, you can reduce risk and increase the potential for long-term returns. Choosing the right investments depends on your investment goals, risk tolerance, and time horizon, and there are different strategies, such as value investing and growth investing, that can be used to choose individual stocks or mutual funds. With a solid understanding of these principles, you can start building a successful investment portfolio and achieving your financial goals.

Benefits of investing

To increase wealth and meet long-term financial objectives, investing can be a potent strategy. While there is always some level of risk involved with investing, the potential rewards can be significant. In this sub-chapter, we will explore some of the key benefits of investing.

Wealth building

One of the most obvious benefits of investing is the potential to build wealth over time. Investing allows you to earn a return on your money, which can then be reinvested to generate even more returns. Over time, these returns can compound, meaning you earn returns not only on your initial investment but also on the returns generated by that investment. For example, let's say you invest $1,000 in a stock that earns a 10% return in the first year. At the end of the year, your investment is worth $1,100. Your investment will be worth $1,210 if you reinvested the $100 return and earned another 10% return the following year. Over time, these compounding returns can add up to significant wealth.

Diversification

Investing also allows you to diversify your assets and reduce risk. You can diversify your risk and lessen the impact of any one investment performing poorly by making investments in a range of different assets, such as stocks, bonds, and real estate. This is known as asset allocation. You can benefit from various market conditions by diversifying your portfolio. For example, if the stock market is experiencing a downturn, you may be able to offset losses in your stock investments with gains in your bond or real estate investments.

Inflation protection

Investing can also be a tool for protecting against inflation. Inflation is the rate at which the general level of prices for goods and services is rising, and over time, inflation can erode the purchasing power of your money. By earning a return on your investments that is greater than the rate of inflation, you can protect the value of your money over time.

Income generation

Investing can also be a source of passive income. By investing in assets such as stocks, bonds, or rental properties, you can earn regular income without having to actively work for it. For example, stocks may pay dividends, bonds may pay interest, and rental properties generate rental income.

Tax benefits

Investing can also offer tax benefits. Certain types of investments, such as 401(k)s or IRAs, offer tax-deferred or tax-free growth, meaning you don't have to pay taxes on your investment gains until you withdraw the money. Additionally, some investments, such as municipal bonds, may offer tax-free income.

Achieving financial goals

Finally, investing can be a powerful tool for achieving long-term financial goals. Whether you're saving for retirement, a child's education, or a down payment on a home, investing can help you reach your goals faster than saving in a traditional savings account. By earning a return on your investments, you can grow your money faster and achieve your financial goals sooner.

In conclusion, investing can offer numerous benefits, including wealth building, diversification, inflation protection, income generation, tax benefits, and the ability to achieve long-term financial goals. While there is always some level of risk involved with investing, the potential rewards can be significant. It's important to do your research, consider your investment goals and risk tolerance, and seek the guidance of a financial professional before investing. With a solid understanding of the benefits of investing and a thoughtful investment strategy, you can start building a successful investment portfolio and achieving your financial goals.

The purpose of the book

The purpose of this book is to provide a comprehensive guide to smart investing and portfolio building for beginners. Investing can be a daunting task, particularly for those who are new to the world of finance. There are countless investment options to choose from, and it can be difficult to know where to start.

This book aims to demystify the world of investing and provide readers with the knowledge and tools they need to make informed investment decisions. We will discuss a variety of subjects, such as:

The basics of investing: We will start by explaining the basics of investing, including the different types of investments available, the risks and rewards of investing, and the importance of diversification.

Building a portfolio: We will then delve into the specifics of building an investment portfolio. We will explain how to determine your investment goals, assess your risk tolerance, and choose the right investments to meet your needs.

Investing strategies: We will explore different investing strategies, including value investing, growth investing, and income investing, and provide guidance on how to choose the right strategy for your needs.

Managing your portfolio: Once you've built your portfolio, we will provide tips on how to manage it effectively. We will cover topics such as rebalancing, monitoring performance, and tax implications.

Common mistakes to avoid: Finally, we will highlight common investing mistakes to avoid, such as chasing hot stocks, ignoring diversification, and trying to time the market.

The goal of this book is to empower readers to take control of their finances and achieve their long-term financial goals through smart investing. By providing clear, concise information and actionable advice, we aim to make investing accessible to everyone, regardless of their level of financial knowledge or experience.

We recognize that investing can be a complex topic, and we aim to present the information in a way that is easy to understand and follow. We will use real-world examples and case studies to illustrate key concepts and provide practical guidance.

Whether you're looking to start investing for the first time, or you're a seasoned investor looking to improve your portfolio, this book has something for you. By following the advice in this book, you can make informed investment decisions, build a successful investment portfolio, and achieve your long-term financial goals.

CHAPTER TWO

THE BASICS OF INVESTING

Investing can be a powerful tool for achieving long-term financial goals, but it can also be overwhelming for beginners. It might be difficult to know where to begin when there are so many financial possibilities available. This is why it is essential to understand the basics of investing. In this section of the book, we will provide an overview of investing, including the different types of investments available, the risks and rewards of investing, and the importance of diversification. By the end of this section, readers will have a solid foundation in the fundamentals of investing and will be better equipped to make informed investment decisions. Whether you're new to investing or looking to refresh your knowledge, this section is a must-read for anyone looking to build a successful investment portfolio.

Definition of investing

Investing is the act of allocating resources, such as money, time, or effort, with the expectation of generating a return in the future. In the context of finance, investing typically refers to the purchase of assets with the expectation of generating income or profit over time.

There are many different types of investments, including stocks, bonds, real estate, and commodities. Each type of investment comes with its own set of risks and potential rewards.

When an individual or organization invests, they are essentially putting their money to work, with the goal of generating a return on their investment. This return can come in the form of capital gains (the increase in the value of the investment over time), dividends (regular payments made by the company to shareholders), or interest payments (payments made on bonds or other fixed-income securities).

Investing can be a powerful tool for achieving long-term financial goals, such as saving for retirement, funding education expenses, or building wealth. However, investing also comes with risks. No investment is completely risk-free, and there is always the possibility of losing money.

To mitigate these risks, it is important to understand the fundamentals of investing and to have a well-diversified investment portfolio. By spreading your investments across a variety of asset classes and investment types, you can reduce the risk of loss and increase the potential for long-term growth.

Overall, investing is a critical component of financial planning and can provide significant benefits over the long-term. However, it is important to approach investing with caution and to seek professional advice when necessary. By understanding the basics of investing and taking a thoughtful approach to portfolio construction, investors can increase their chances of success and achieve their financial goals.

Stocks, bonds, mutual funds, ETFs, and other types of investments

When it comes to investing, there are many different types of investments to choose from. Each type of investment comes with its own set of risks and potential rewards, and it's important to understand the characteristics of each type of investment in order to make informed investment decisions. In this section, we'll take a closer look at some of the most common types of investments, including stocks, bonds, mutual funds, ETFs, and more.

Stocks: A stock represents ownership in a company, and when you purchase a stock, you are essentially buying a piece of that company. Stocks are traded on stock exchanges, and their value can fluctuate based on a variety of factors, including the company's financial performance, news events, and broader economic trends. Stocks are generally considered to be a higher-risk investment, but they also offer the potential for higher returns over the long term.

Bonds: A bond is a type of debt security issued by a company or government. When you purchase a bond, you are essentially lending money to the issuer, who promises to pay back the principal plus interest over a set period of time. Bonds are generally considered to be a lower-risk investment than stocks, but they also offer lower potential returns.

Mutual funds are a form of investment instrument that aggregate the funds of numerous individuals to buy a diverse portfolio of stocks, bonds, or other assets. By investing in a mutual fund, you can benefit from diversification without having to purchase individual stocks or bonds. Mutual funds are typically managed by professional fund managers, who make investment decisions on behalf of the fund's investors. Mutual funds can be either actively managed or passively managed, and they can be structured in a variety of ways, such as index funds, bond funds, or sector funds.

ETFs: An exchange-traded fund (ETF) is similar to a mutual fund in that it pools money from multiple investors to purchase a diversified portfolio of assets. However, ETFs are traded on stock exchanges like individual stocks, and they can be bought and sold throughout the trading day. ETFs can be structured in a variety of ways, such as index ETFs, bond ETFs, or commodity ETFs.

Real estate: Real estate investing involves purchasing physical property, such as a rental property or commercial building, with the goal of generating rental income and/or capital gains. Real estate can be a high-risk investment, as it often requires a significant amount of upfront capital and can be subject to market fluctuations. However, it can also offer significant potential rewards, such as passive income and long-term appreciation.

Alternative investments: Alternative investments are any type of investment that does not fit into the traditional categories of stocks, bonds, or real estate. Hedge funds, private equity, fine art, and collectibles are a few examples of alternative investments. Alternative investments can be high-risk, high-reward investments, and they are typically only available to accredited investors who meet certain income or net worth requirements.

Each type of investment comes with its own set of risks and potential rewards, and it's important to consider your personal investment goals, risk tolerance, and investment horizon when selecting the investments to include in your portfolio. Diversification across multiple asset classes and investment types can help to reduce overall risk and increase potential returns over the long term. By understanding the characteristics of different types of investments and taking a thoughtful approach to portfolio construction, investors can increase their chances of achieving their financial goals.

Understanding risk and return

There is always a trade-off between risk and profit in investment. In general, the higher the potential return of an investment, the higher the risk that investment carries. Conversely, investments with lower potential returns typically carry lower levels of risk. Understanding the relationship between risk and return is essential for building a well-balanced investment portfolio that meets your financial goals and risk tolerance.

Risk: In the context of investing, risk refers to the possibility that you will lose some or all of your investment. There are many different types of investment risk, including market risk, inflation risk, interest rate risk, credit risk, and more. Market risk is perhaps the most well-known type of investment risk, and it refers to the possibility that the value of your investments will decline due to market fluctuations, such as changes in stock prices or bond yields. Inflation risk is the possibility that the purchasing power of your investments will be eroded over time due to inflation. Interest rate risk is the possibility that changes in interest rates will affect the value of your fixed-income investments, such as bonds.

Return: Return refers to the amount of money you earn on your investment, expressed as a percentage of the initial investment. The potential return of an investment depends on a variety of factors, including the type of investment, the level of risk, and the investment horizon. In general, investments with higher levels of risk offer the potential for higher returns over the long term, while lower-risk investments typically offer lower potential returns.

Risk tolerance: Risk tolerance refers to your willingness and ability to take on investment risk. Some investors are comfortable taking on higher levels of risk in order to achieve higher potential returns, while others prefer to stick to lower-risk investments even if it means potentially lower returns. Understanding your risk tolerance is essential for building a well-balanced investment portfolio that meets your financial goals and personal preferences.

The practice of distributing your financial portfolio among several asset classes, such as stocks, bonds, and cash, is known as asset allocation. The goal of asset allocation is to achieve a balance between risk and return by investing in a mix of assets that aligns with your risk tolerance and financial goals. For example, a young investor with a long investment horizon and a high risk tolerance may choose to allocate a larger percentage of their portfolio to stocks, while an older investor with a shorter investment horizon and a lower risk tolerance may choose to allocate a larger percentage of their portfolio to bonds.

Diversification: Diversification is the practice of spreading your investment portfolio across a variety of different assets and asset classes in order to reduce overall risk. You can lessen the effect of any one investment on your portfolio's performance overall by diversifying your holdings. For example, if you invest all of your money in a single stock, you are exposed to the specific risks of that company, such as poor financial performance or negative news events. However, if you diversify your portfolio across multiple stocks, bonds, and other assets, you can reduce the impact of any one investment on your overall portfolio performance.

Rebalancing is the process of occasionally modifying your investment portfolio to preserve your intended asset allocation. As some assets perform better than others over time, your portfolio can become unbalanced, which can increase your overall risk. By rebalancing your portfolio, you can ensure that your investments continue to align with your risk tolerance and financial goals.

Investing involves a certain degree of risk, and it's important to understand the different types of risks that are associated with different types of investments. Market risk, as mentioned earlier, is the risk that the value of your investments will decline due to market fluctuations. This type of risk can be mitigated through diversification and asset allocation, but it can never be completely eliminated. Inflation risk, on the other hand, is the risk that the purchasing power of your investments will be eroded over time due to inflation. Inflation risk can be mitigated by investing in assets that have historically kept pace with or outpaced inflation, such as stocks or real estate.

Interest rate risk is the risk that changes in interest rates will affect the value of your fixed-income investments, such as bonds. When interest rates rise, the value of existing bonds declines, as new bonds are issued at higher interest rates, making existing bonds less attractive to investors. This can be mitigated by investing in a mix of fixed-income investments with different maturities, so that as some bonds mature, they can be reinvested in new bonds with higher interest rates.

Credit risk is the risk that a borrower will default on their loan or bond payments, resulting in a loss of principal and interest for the investor. This type of risk can be mitigated by investing in high-quality bonds or funds that invest in high-quality bonds, as these are less likely to default.

When it comes to returns, there are no guarantees. Investments with higher potential returns typically carry higher levels of risk, but there is no guarantee that you will achieve those returns. Conversely, investments with lower potential returns typically carry lower levels of risk, but may not provide the level of returns you need to meet your financial goals. It's important to consider both risk and return when building your investment portfolio.

Asset allocation and diversification are two key principles for mitigating risk in your investment portfolio. To create a balance between risk and return, asset allocation entails splitting your portfolio among several asset types, such as stocks, bonds, and cash. Diversification involves spreading your portfolio across a variety of different investments within each asset class to reduce the impact of any one investment on your overall portfolio performance. By investing in a mix of assets and spreading your investments across different sectors, industries, and geographies, you can reduce the impact of any one investment on your overall portfolio performance.

Rebalancing is also an important principle for maintaining a well-balanced investment portfolio. As some investments perform better than others over time, your portfolio can become unbalanced, which can increase your overall risk. By periodically adjusting your portfolio to maintain your desired asset allocation, you can ensure that your investments continue to align with your risk tolerance and financial goals.

Overall, understanding risk and return is essential for building a well-balanced investment portfolio that meets your financial goals and risk tolerance. By considering the different types of investment risk, your risk tolerance, and the principles of asset allocation, diversification, and rebalancing, you can build a portfolio that aligns with your personal preferences and helps you achieve your long-term financial goals.

How the stock market works

The stock market is a complex and dynamic system that facilitates the buying and selling of shares of publicly traded companies. Understanding how the stock market works is crucial for investors who want to participate in the market and make informed investment decisions.

At its most basic level, the stock market is a marketplace where buyers and sellers come together to exchange shares of ownership in publicly traded companies. When a company goes public, it sells shares of its ownership to the public in the form of stocks. These stocks are then bought and sold on stock exchanges, such as the New York Stock Exchange (NYSE) and NASDAQ.

The laws of supply and demand govern how the stock market works. When there is a high demand for a particular stock, its price goes up, and when there is a low demand, its price goes down. The price of a stock is determined by the market participants who are buying and selling the stock, based on their assessment of the company's future prospects.

Stock prices are also influenced by a variety of other factors, including economic indicators, news events, and company-specific information such as earnings reports and management changes. For example, if a company announces better-than-expected earnings, its stock price may increase, as investors perceive that the company is performing well and is likely to continue to do so in the future.

Investors can buy and sell stocks through a brokerage firm, either online or through a traditional brick-and-mortar office. When an investor places an order to buy or sell a stock, the brokerage firm facilitates the transaction by matching the buyer with a seller or vice versa. The brokerage firm charges a fee or commission for its services, which can vary depending on the type of account and the level of service provided.

Investors can also participate in the stock market through mutual funds, exchange-traded funds (ETFs), and other investment vehicles. These funds allow investors to buy a diversified portfolio of stocks or other assets with a single investment, making it easier to manage risk and achieve a desired level of diversification.

In addition to the primary market where stocks are initially issued, there is also a secondary market where previously issued stocks are bought and sold. The secondary market is where most stock trading takes place, and it is where investors can buy and sell stocks on a daily basis.

The stock market is a highly regulated industry, with rules and regulations designed to protect investors and ensure fair and transparent trading. The Securities and Exchange Commission (SEC) is the primary regulator of the stock market in the United States, and it oversees everything from financial reporting requirements to insider trading regulations.

Overall, the stock market is a complex and ever-evolving system that is influenced by a wide variety of factors. Understanding how the stock market works is crucial for investors who want to participate in the market and make informed investment decisions. By staying up-to-date on market trends and developments and by working with a trusted financial advisor or brokerage firm, investors can navigate the stock market with confidence and achieve their long-term financial goals.

CHAPTER THREE

GETTING STARTED

Congratulations on taking the first step towards investing! Getting started can be both exciting and intimidating, especially if you're new to the world of investing. But don't worry - this section will guide you through the process of getting started with investing and building your investment portfolio.

In this section, we will cover the essential steps you need to take to start investing, including setting investment goals, understanding your risk tolerance, choosing an investment account, and building a diversified portfolio. We will also provide tips on how to stay on track and make adjustments to your portfolio as needed.

Whether you're saving for retirement, planning for a major purchase, or just looking to grow your wealth, investing can help you achieve your financial goals. If you have the right approach and strategy, you can succeed as an investor. So let's get started!

Setting investment goals

Before you start investing, it's essential to set clear investment goals. Investment goals help you define your objectives and create a roadmap for your investment strategy. Setting investment goals will help you determine how much money you need to invest, what type of investment products you should consider, and how long you should invest.

The first step in setting investment goals is to identify your financial objectives. Your financial objectives could be long-term or short-term, and they should be specific, measurable, and realistic. Examples of long-term financial goals include saving for retirement, paying off debt, or purchasing a home. Short-term goals might include building an emergency fund, taking a vacation, or buying a new car.

Once you've identified your financial objectives, you should determine how much money you need to achieve each goal. It's important to be realistic about your financial situation and your ability to save and invest. Don't set goals that are too high and don't consider your current income, expenses, and savings habits. Instead, be honest with yourself about your financial situation and set realistic goals that you can achieve over time.

Once you've determined your financial objectives and how much money you need to invest, you should decide on a time horizon for each goal. Your time horizon is the amount of time you have to achieve your financial objectives. It's important to consider your age, risk tolerance, and investment goals when deciding on a time horizon. Generally, long-term goals require a longer time horizon than short-term goals.

Finally, you should consider your risk tolerance when setting investment goals. Your risk tolerance is your ability to tolerate market volatility and fluctuations in the value of your investments. If you have a low risk tolerance, you may want to consider investing in less risky investments, such as bonds or mutual funds. If you have a high risk tolerance, you may be comfortable investing in more aggressive investments, such as stocks or exchange-traded funds (ETFs).

In summary, setting investment goals is an essential step in the investment process. Your investment goals should be specific, measurable, and realistic, and you should consider your financial objectives, time horizon, and risk tolerance when setting them. Once you've set your investment goals, you can begin developing an investment strategy that will help you achieve your financial objectives over time.

Assessing risk tolerance

Assessing your risk tolerance is an essential step in the investment process. Your risk tolerance is your ability to tolerate market volatility and fluctuations in the value of your investments. Understanding your risk tolerance is critical because it will help you choose the appropriate investments that align with your investment goals.

To assess your risk tolerance, you must consider your financial situation, investment goals, and personal preferences. Several factors can affect your risk tolerance, including your age, income, expenses, savings habits, and investment experience.

One way to assess your risk tolerance is to complete a risk tolerance questionnaire. Risk tolerance questionnaires are typically offered by investment advisors, financial planners, or online brokerage firms. These questionnaires ask a series of questions about your investment objectives, time horizon, financial situation, and personal preferences. Based on your responses, the questionnaire will assign a risk score that reflects your risk tolerance.

Another way to assess your risk tolerance is to evaluate your reactions to market fluctuations. If you become anxious or stressed when the value of your investments declines, you may have a low risk tolerance. On the other hand, if you can tolerate market volatility and remain calm during downturns, you may have a high risk tolerance.

It's important to note that risk tolerance is not static and can change over time. Your risk tolerance may change due to changes in your financial situation, investment goals, or personal circumstances. For example, as you near retirement, you may become more risk-averse and prefer less risky investments to protect your savings.

Once you've assessed your risk tolerance, you can begin to select investments that align with your risk tolerance and investment goals. If you have a low risk tolerance, you may prefer to invest in less risky investments such as bonds or mutual funds. These investments offer lower returns but are generally less volatile than stocks. If you have a high risk tolerance, you may be comfortable investing in more aggressive investments such as stocks or exchange-traded funds (ETFs). These investments offer higher returns but are generally more volatile than bonds.

In summary, assessing your risk tolerance is a critical step in the investment process. Your risk tolerance is your ability to tolerate market volatility and fluctuations in the value of your investments. To assess your risk tolerance, you can complete a risk tolerance questionnaire or evaluate your reactions to market fluctuations. Your risk tolerance may change over time due to changes in your financial situation, investment goals, or personal circumstances. Once you've assessed your risk tolerance, you can begin to select investments that align with your investment goals and risk tolerance.

Creating a budget

Creating a budget is a crucial step in managing your finances and achieving your financial goals, including investing. A budget is simply a plan that outlines your income and expenses for a specific period, typically a month. The purpose of a budget is to help you understand how you're spending your money and to identify areas where you can save or cut back. By creating a budget, you can free up money to invest, pay off debt, or save for other financial goals.

To create a budget, you'll need to gather information about your income and expenses. Start by reviewing your bank and credit card statements for the past few months to identify your regular expenses, including rent or mortgage payments, utilities, groceries, transportation, and entertainment. Include all unforeseen costs, including those for car repairs or medical expenditures.

Next, calculate your monthly income, including your salary, wages, bonuses, and any other sources of income. Subtract your total expenses from your total income to determine your monthly net income. If your expenses exceed your income, you may need to find ways to cut back or increase your income to balance your budget.

Once you've determined your net income, allocate your expenses into categories, such as housing, transportation, and entertainment. Set a budget for each category based on your past spending patterns and your financial goals. For example, if you want to invest $500 per month, you may need to cut back on your entertainment budget to free up the money.

It's crucial to frequently check your budget to make sure you're on course and moving closer to your financial objectives. Make adjustments as needed, such as reducing expenses or increasing your income, to ensure you're meeting your financial objectives.

Creating a budget can seem daunting at first, but it's a vital step in managing your finances and achieving your financial goals. By understanding your income and expenses and making a plan to manage your money, you can free up money to invest and take control of your financial future.

Building an emergency fund

An emergency fund is an essential component of any financial plan, including investing. An emergency fund is a reserve of money set aside to cover unexpected expenses, such as a medical emergency, car repair, or job loss. Without an emergency fund, unexpected expenses can derail your financial goals, including your investment plans.

Building an emergency fund should be a priority, even before you start investing. Three to six months' worth of living expenses should be set aside in an emergency fund as a general guideline. However, the amount you need may vary depending on your individual circumstances, such as job stability, family size, and monthly expenses.

To start building an emergency fund, set a savings goal based on your estimated monthly living expenses. Open a separate savings account specifically for your emergency fund to avoid spending the money on non-emergency expenses. To make saving easier, think about automating transfers from your checking account to your emergency fund savings account.

While building an emergency fund may seem daunting, it's important to start small and be consistent. Even saving $25 per week can add up to over $1,000 in a year. Focus on creating a habit of saving regularly and gradually increasing your savings over time.

It's important to keep your emergency fund easily accessible in case of an emergency, so consider keeping it in a high-yield savings account or money market account. Avoid investing your emergency fund in the stock market or other high-risk investments that may lose value when you need the money.

Once you've built an emergency fund, continue to contribute to it regularly, even as you begin investing. Remember that unexpected expenses can still arise, even as you work toward your financial goals. Having an emergency fund can provide peace of mind and financial security, allowing you to focus on your long-term investment plans.

In summary, building an emergency fund is a crucial step in any financial plan, including investing. By setting a savings goal, creating a habit of saving regularly, and keeping your emergency fund easily accessible, you can prepare for unexpected expenses and stay on track toward your financial goals. Remember, investing is a long-term strategy, and having an emergency fund can provide the security and peace of mind needed to stay the course.

CHAPTER FOUR

BUILDING A PORTFOLIO

Building a portfolio is a critical step in the investment process. A portfolio is a collection of investments, such as stocks, bonds, mutual funds, or ETFs, that are designed to meet an individual's investment goals while managing risk. By diversifying your investments across different asset classes and industries, you can potentially increase your returns while reducing your risk. In this section, we'll explore the key concepts and strategies for building a diversified investment portfolio that aligns with your goals and risk tolerance.

Asset allocation and diversification

Asset allocation and diversification are two key principles in building a successful investment portfolio. Asset allocation refers to the process of dividing your investments among different asset classes, such as stocks, bonds, and cash equivalents, while diversification involves spreading your investments within each asset class across various companies and industries. The goal of asset allocation and diversification is to minimize risk while maximizing returns.

Asset allocation is an important factor in determining the overall risk and return of your portfolio. Each asset class has its own level of risk and potential return. Stocks, for example, tend to offer higher potential returns than bonds but also carry a higher level of risk. Cash equivalents, such as savings accounts and money market funds, offer low potential returns but are considered to be the safest investment option. By diversifying your investments across different asset classes, you can balance your risk and return to achieve your investment objectives.

When determining your asset allocation, it's important to consider your investment goals, risk tolerance, and time horizon. If you have a long time horizon and a higher risk tolerance, you may choose to allocate a larger portion of your portfolio to stocks. On the other hand, if you have a shorter time horizon or a lower risk tolerance, you may opt for a more conservative allocation with a larger percentage of your portfolio in bonds or cash equivalents.

Diversification involves spreading your investments within each asset class across different companies and industries. The goal is to minimize the risk associated with investing in any single company or industry. By diversifying your investments, you can potentially reduce the impact of market fluctuations and protect your portfolio from significant losses.

There are several ways to diversify your portfolio. One method is to invest in mutual funds or exchange-traded funds (ETFs), which allow you to own a diversified portfolio of stocks or bonds without having to purchase each security individually. Another way to diversify is to invest in a mix of large-cap, mid-cap, and small-cap stocks. You may also choose to invest in international stocks or bonds to diversify across geographic regions.

Another important aspect of diversification is asset class diversification. Within each asset class, it's important to diversify across different subcategories. For example, in the bond market, you may want to diversify across different types of bonds, such as government, corporate, and municipal bonds. In the stock market, you may want to diversify across different industries, such as technology, healthcare, and financials.

While diversification can help reduce risk, it's important to note that it does not guarantee a profit or protect against losses in a declining market. It's important to regularly review and adjust your portfolio to ensure that it remains aligned with your investment goals and risk tolerance.

In conclusion, asset allocation and diversification are critical components of building a successful investment portfolio. By spreading your investments across different asset classes and industries, you can balance risk and return and potentially achieve your investment objectives. To make sure that your portfolio stays in line with your objectives and risk tolerance, it's critical to monitor and make adjustments on a frequent basis.

Stock vs. bond allocation

When building a portfolio, one of the critical decisions to make is how much to allocate to stocks and how much to bonds. This allocation is a crucial aspect of asset allocation and diversification.

Stocks and bonds have different characteristics that make them suitable for different types of investors and investment goals. In contrast to bonds, which reflect debt issued by a firm or government, stocks indicate ownership in a company. Stocks are generally considered riskier than bonds but have higher potential for returns over the long term. Bonds are generally considered safer but have lower potential for returns over the long term.

When it comes to deciding how much of your portfolio to allocate to stocks versus bonds, there are several factors to consider. One is your investment horizon, or how long you plan to hold your investments. Generally, the longer your investment horizon, the more you can afford to allocate to stocks. This is because stocks tend to provide higher returns over the long term, although they can be volatile in the short term. If you have a shorter investment horizon, you may want to allocate more to bonds, which are less volatile and provide more stable returns.

Another factor to consider is your risk tolerance, or how comfortable you are with taking on risk. If you have a high risk tolerance, you may be comfortable with a higher allocation to stocks, as you are willing to accept more volatility in exchange for potentially higher returns. If you have a low risk tolerance, you may prefer a higher allocation to bonds, which are generally less volatile and provide more stability.

Your investment goals are also an essential consideration when deciding how to allocate your portfolio between stocks and bonds. If your goal is to preserve capital and generate income, you may want to allocate more to bonds, which are generally considered safer and provide more stable returns. If your goal is to achieve growth and higher returns, you may want to allocate more to stocks, which have higher potential for long-term growth.

It's important to remember that asset allocation is not a one-time decision. As your investment horizon, risk tolerance, and investment goals change, you may need to adjust your portfolio's allocation between stocks and bonds. Regularly reviewing and rebalancing your portfolio can help ensure that it remains aligned with your investment objectives.

When it comes to investing in stocks and bonds, there are several options to consider. One option is to invest in individual stocks or bonds, which allows you to handpick your investments and tailor your portfolio to your specific goals and preferences. However, this approach requires a significant amount of research and expertise and can be time-consuming and costly.

Another option is to invest in mutual funds or exchange-traded funds (ETFs), which offer a more diversified approach to investing in stocks and bonds. These funds pool money from multiple investors and invest in a variety of stocks or bonds, providing instant diversification and professional management. Mutual funds and ETFs are available in a range of investment styles and asset classes, making it easy to build a diversified portfolio that aligns with your investment goals and risk tolerance.

In summary, the allocation of stocks versus bonds is a crucial aspect of building a portfolio. The allocation should be based on factors such as investment horizon, risk tolerance, and investment goals. Investors have the option to invest in individual stocks and bonds or use mutual funds and ETFs to gain instant diversification and professional management. Regularly reviewing and rebalancing your portfolio can help ensure that it remains aligned with your investment objectives over time.

Choosing individual stocks and bonds

When building an investment portfolio, one of the most important decisions an investor must make is whether to invest in individual stocks and bonds or to use mutual funds or exchange-traded funds (ETFs) that hold a diversified mix of securities.

Investing in individual stocks and bonds requires significant research and analysis, but can offer the potential for higher returns. When investing in individual stocks, it's important to consider factors such as the company's financial health, management team, industry trends, and competition. Investors may also look at a company's price-to-earnings ratio (P/E ratio), dividend yield, and earnings growth potential when deciding whether to invest.

Bonds, on the other hand, are debt securities issued by companies or governments to raise funds. When investing in bonds, investors should consider factors such as credit ratings, maturity dates, and interest rates. Higher-rated bonds generally have lower yields, but are less risky than lower-rated bonds. Bond prices tend to move inversely with interest rates, so it's important to consider the current interest rate environment when investing in bonds.

While investing in individual stocks and bonds offers the potential for higher returns, it also carries a higher degree of risk. If an individual company or bond issuer experiences financial difficulty, the investor could suffer significant losses. To mitigate this risk, investors may choose to invest in a diversified mix of stocks and bonds.

Investors may also choose to invest in mutual funds or ETFs, which hold a diversified mix of securities. These funds are managed by professional fund managers who select and manage the underlying securities. This can be a more hands-off approach to investing, as the investor is not responsible for selecting individual securities. Instead, the fund manager makes investment decisions based on the fund's investment objective.

Mutual funds and ETFs can be a good option for investors who want a diversified portfolio without having to spend significant time researching individual securities. Additionally, mutual funds and ETFs offer investors the ability to invest in a broad range of asset classes, including stocks, bonds, and alternative investments such as real estate or commodities.

When selecting mutual funds or ETFs, it's important to consider factors such as the fund's investment objective, historical performance, fees, and fund manager. Additionally, investors should consider the fund's asset allocation to ensure that it aligns with their investment goals and risk tolerance.

Overall, the decision to invest in individual stocks and bonds or mutual funds and ETFs ultimately depends on an investor's goals, risk tolerance, and investment strategy. While investing in individual securities requires more research and analysis, it also offers the potential for higher returns. Investing in mutual funds and ETFs, on the other hand, offers a more diversified approach to investing, but may not offer the same potential for high returns. By considering these factors and selecting an investment strategy that aligns with their goals, investors can build a well-diversified portfolio that meets their individual needs.

Investing in mutual funds and ETFs

Investing in mutual funds and exchange-traded funds (ETFs) can be a great way to diversify your portfolio and gain exposure to a wide range of assets with relatively low cost and effort. These investment vehicles are popular among both beginner and experienced investors due to their many benefits, including ease of access, professional management, and instant diversification. In this section, we'll explore the basics of mutual funds and ETFs, how they differ, and what factors to consider when choosing between them.

What are mutual funds?

A mutual fund is a particular kind of investment instrument that collects funds from numerous people and utilizes those funds to purchase a portfolio of various assets, including stocks, bonds, and cash. Each investor in the mutual fund owns a share of the fund and is entitled to a portion of the fund's returns based on the number of shares owned. Mutual funds are typically managed by professional fund managers who make investment decisions on behalf of the investors in the fund.

Mutual funds offer several benefits to investors. One key benefit is diversification. By investing in a mutual fund, an investor gains exposure to a broad range of assets, which can help reduce overall portfolio risk. Additionally, mutual funds can be an affordable way to access professional management and research, which can be especially valuable for those who lack the expertise or time to manage their investments themselves.

What are ETFs?

ETFs are similar to mutual funds in that they provide investors with exposure to a diversified portfolio of assets. However, there are some key differences between the two investment vehicles. Unlike mutual funds, which are priced at the end of each trading day based on the net asset value (NAV) of the fund, ETFs trade on exchanges throughout the day like individual stocks. This means that ETF prices can fluctuate more frequently than mutual funds, but also that they offer greater flexibility for investors who want to buy or sell shares throughout the trading day.

ETFs also tend to have lower fees than mutual funds, which can make them an attractive option for cost-conscious investors. Additionally, ETFs offer tax efficiency, as investors can buy and sell shares without triggering capital gains taxes until they actually sell the ETF shares.

Choosing between mutual funds and ETFs

When deciding between mutual funds and ETFs, there are several factors to consider. One important factor is the cost. While ETFs tend to have lower fees than mutual funds, the exact cost will depend on the specific fund and its management style. Additionally, it's important to consider the trading costs associated with buying and selling ETF shares, as these can add up over time.

Another factor to consider is the investment strategy of the fund. Some funds are actively managed, which means that a seasoned fund manager makes investment choices on the investors' behalf. Other funds are passively managed and seek to track the performance of a specific index or benchmark. Passive funds tend to have lower fees than actively managed funds, but may not offer the same level of potential returns.

Investors should also consider the overall risk and return profile of the fund, as well as the underlying assets that the fund invests in. For example, a fund that invests heavily in technology stocks may be more volatile than a fund that invests in a broad range of assets across different sectors.

Mutual funds and ETFs can be excellent investment vehicles for those looking to diversify their portfolio and gain exposure to a wide range of assets. Both types of funds offer benefits such as professional management, diversification, and low cost. However, it's important to consider the specific features and investment strategy of each fund before making an investment decision. By understanding the basics of mutual funds and ETFs, investors can make informed decisions that align with their investment goals and risk tolerance.

The importance of low fees

When it comes to investing, fees can have a significant impact on your overall returns. This is because fees, such as expense ratios and transaction fees, reduce the amount of money you have working for you in your portfolio.

Expense ratios are the annual fees charged by mutual funds and ETFs to cover their operating expenses. These fees are expressed as a percentage of your investment, and can range from less than 0.10% for some index funds to over 2% for some actively managed funds. While it may not seem like a big difference, the impact of these fees can be significant over the long term.

Consider two investors who each invest $10,000 in different mutual funds. One fund charges an expense ratio of 0.10% per year, while the other charges 1.00% per year. Assuming both funds earn an average annual return of 7%, after 30 years, the investor in the fund with the lower expense ratio would have a portfolio value of approximately $58,000, while the investor in the fund with the higher expense ratio would have a portfolio value of approximately $44,000. That's a difference of $14,000, or 24% less in returns, simply due to the higher fees.

Transaction fees, also known as brokerage fees or trading fees, are charged by brokers when you buy or sell stocks, bonds, mutual funds, and ETFs. These fees can vary widely depending on the broker and the type of investment you are buying or selling. Some brokers charge a flat fee per trade, while others charge a percentage of the transaction amount.

Transaction fees can add up quickly, particularly if you are an active trader. For example, if your broker charges a $10 commission per trade and you make 100 trades per year, you'll pay $1,000 in transaction fees alone. This is money that could have been invested in your portfolio instead.

In addition to expense ratios and transaction fees, there may be other fees associated with your investments, such as account maintenance fees, account closing fees, and early redemption fees. These fees can also eat into your returns, so it's important to be aware of all the costs associated with your investments.

To minimize the impact of fees on your portfolio, it's important to choose low-cost investments, such as index funds and ETFs, and to be mindful of transaction fees when buying and selling investments. By keeping your costs low, you'll be able to keep more of your returns working for you in your portfolio, which can help you achieve your long-term investment goals.

CHAPTER FIVE

INVESTMENT STRATEGIES

Investment strategies are plans that guide investors on how to allocate their resources to achieve specific investment goals. These tactics aim to reduce risks while maximizing returns. There are several investment strategies available to investors, and selecting the right one can be a daunting task.

This section of the book will provide a comprehensive overview of various investment strategies and their suitability for different types of investors. It will also highlight the benefits and drawbacks of each strategy to help readers make informed investment decisions. By the end of this section, readers will be equipped with the knowledge and tools needed to develop and implement an effective investment strategy that aligns with their goals, risk tolerance, and investment horizon.

Value investing

Value investing is an investment strategy that involves identifying and investing in undervalued companies. These are companies whose stocks are trading at a price lower than their intrinsic value. The goal of value investing is to buy these undervalued stocks, hold them for an extended period, and sell them when the market recognizes their true worth, resulting in significant returns.

The concept of value investing was popularized by Benjamin Graham, a legendary investor and Warren Buffet's mentor. Graham believed that investing in undervalued stocks was the best way to achieve long-term success in the stock market. He emphasized the importance of fundamental analysis in identifying undervalued companies and encouraged investors to buy stocks trading at a discount to their intrinsic value.

The fundamental analysis used in value investing involves analysing a company's financial statements, including the income statement, balance sheet, and cash flow statement.

The analysis aims to identify companies with strong financials, stable earnings, and a competitive advantage over their peers.

In addition to fundamental analysis, value investors also use other metrics to identify undervalued stocks. These include the price-to-earnings ratio (P/E ratio), price-to-book ratio (P/B ratio), and dividend yield. A company with a low P/E or P/B ratio compared to its peers is likely undervalued, and its stock is a potential value investment.

Value investing is a long-term tactic that calls for restraint and patience. Value investors must be willing to hold on to their investments for an extended period, even if the market is not performing as expected. The strategy is also not without risks. Companies that are undervalued may not always rebound as expected, resulting in losses for investors.

One of the most famous value investors is Warren Buffet, who has used this strategy to amass a fortune. Buffet's investment philosophy is based on finding undervalued stocks and holding them for the long-term. He believes that investing in high-quality companies at a reasonable price is the key to long-term success in the stock market.

Value investing has proven to be a successful investment strategy over the years. However, it requires a considerable amount of time, effort, and knowledge to implement successfully. Investors must be willing to do their research, analyse financial statements, and monitor their investments regularly.

In conclusion, value investing is an investment strategy that involves identifying and investing in undervalued companies. It requires a significant amount of effort and knowledge to implement successfully, but it has proven to be a successful long-term investment strategy. By understanding the fundamental analysis and other metrics used in value investing, investors can identify undervalued stocks and potentially reap significant returns.

Growth investing

Growth investing is an investment strategy that involves buying stocks of companies with the potential for above-average growth in earnings or revenue. Investors who follow this strategy are willing to pay a premium for the stock in anticipation of future growth. The main goal of growth investing is to generate capital gains, which means selling the stocks at a higher price than the purchase price.

The idea behind growth investing is simple. Companies that are growing rapidly are more likely to have a strong future than those that are not. These companies tend to have high earnings growth rates, which in turn lead to higher stock prices. Growth investors look for companies that have a strong track record of growth, innovative products or services, and a competitive advantage in their respective markets.

Growth investment is a long-term approach that necessitates patience and self-control. Investors need to be willing to hold onto their investments for several years to realize significant gains. It is also important to note that not all growth stocks are created equal. Some growth companies may have a high level of risk associated with them, while others may be more stable.

Investors who are interested in growth investing should consider a few key factors before making any investments. First, they should consider the company's financials, such as revenue growth, earnings growth, and profitability. Second, they should look at the company's competitive position in its industry and consider whether it has a sustainable competitive advantage. Third, they should consider the valuation of the stock and whether it is trading at a reasonable price relative to its earnings growth potential.

One of the main benefits of growth investing is the potential for significant capital gains. Growth stocks can experience explosive price increases as the company's earnings grow. For example, if a growth company's earnings grow at a rate of 20% per year, the company's stock price could double in just four years. This potential for significant capital gains is why many investors are attracted to growth investing.

However, growth investing does come with its share of risks. Companies that are growing rapidly are often more volatile and can experience sharp price declines if their growth slows down or if the company fails to meet investors' high expectations. This is why it is important for investors to have a diversified portfolio that includes both growth and value stocks, as well as other asset classes such as bonds and cash.

In summary, growth investing is a long-term investment strategy that involves buying stocks of companies with high growth potential. While it can lead to significant capital gains, it also comes with its share of risks. Investors should carefully consider a company's financials, competitive position, and valuation before making any investments. Additionally, investors should have a well-diversified portfolio that includes both growth and value stocks, as well as other asset classes.

Income investing

Income investing is an investment strategy that focuses on generating a regular stream of income through investments that offer a consistent and predictable yield. This strategy is particularly attractive to investors who are looking to generate passive income or supplement their retirement income.

The main goal of income investing is to build a portfolio of assets that generates a steady stream of income, typically in the form of dividends, interest payments, or rental income. These assets can include bonds, dividend-paying stocks, real estate investment trusts (REITs), and other income-generating securities.

One of the key benefits of income investing is the potential for stable and predictable returns. Unlike growth investing, which focuses on capital appreciation, income investing prioritizes steady income generation. This can help to provide a stable source of cash flow that can be used to cover living expenses, reinvested for growth, or used to achieve other financial goals.

Another benefit of income investing is the potential for diversification. By investing in a range of income-generating assets, investors can spread their risk across different asset classes and reduce their exposure to any one particular investment. This can help to lessen the effects of market changes and offer a more stable investing environment.

When considering an income investment, it is important to pay attention to the yield and risk associated with the investment. The yield represents the amount of income generated by the investment, expressed as a percentage of the initial investment. Higher yields may be more attractive, but they often come with higher risk, such as a higher chance of default on bonds or lower growth potential for stocks.

It is also important to consider the overall risk profile of the investment. While income investing is generally considered a lower-risk strategy, it is not without risk. For example, bonds are subject to interest rate risk, which can cause the value of the bond to decline if interest rates rise. Similarly, dividend-paying stocks may be more volatile than non-dividend-paying stocks.

There are several different approaches to income investing, each with its own advantages and disadvantages. Some investors may prefer a more conservative approach, focusing on low-risk, fixed-income investments such as government bonds or certificates of deposit (CDs). Others may be more comfortable with higher-risk investments, such as high-yield bonds or dividend-paying stocks.

One popular approach to income investing is the dividend growth strategy. This approach focuses on investing in companies that have a history of consistently increasing their dividend payments over time. By investing in these companies, investors can benefit from both the regular income generated by the dividends and the potential for capital appreciation as the company continues to grow.

Another approach to income investing is the bond ladder strategy. This strategy involves investing in a series of bonds with varying maturity dates. By staggered the maturity dates, investors can create a predictable stream of income while also minimizing interest rate risk.

Ultimately, the best approach to income investing will depend on the investor's individual goals, risk tolerance, and financial situation. It is important to carefully consider all options and consult with a financial advisor before making any investment decisions.

Index investing

Index investing is a passive investment strategy that involves investing in an index fund or exchange-traded fund (ETF) that tracks a particular market index, such as the S&P 500 or the Dow Jones Industrial Average. The goal of index investing is to achieve the same returns as the overall market while minimizing costs and risks associated with active management.

The concept of index investing was first introduced by John C. Bogle, founder of The Vanguard Group, who created the first index fund, the Vanguard 500 Index Fund, in 1976. Since then, index investing has become increasingly popular among investors due to its simplicity, low cost, and potential for long-term returns.

Index investing is based on the efficient market hypothesis, which suggests that it is difficult for individual investors or professional fund managers to consistently outperform the market by selecting individual stocks or timing the market. Instead, the hypothesis suggests that it is more efficient to invest in the overall market and earn the average return.

Index funds and ETFs that track market indexes are designed to replicate the performance of the underlying index by holding the same stocks in the same proportions as the index. For example, an S&P 500 index fund would hold the 500 stocks in the S&P 500 index in the same proportion as the index.

The low cost of index investing is one of its key benefits. Because index funds and ETFs are passively managed, they do not require the same level of research and analysis as actively managed funds, which can result in lower management fees and operating expenses. This can translate to higher returns for investors over the long term.

In addition to low cost, index investing also provides diversification benefits. By investing in a broad market index, investors are exposed to a diverse range of companies and industries, which can help reduce the risk associated with individual stock selection. This can be particularly beneficial for investors who do not have the time or expertise to research and select individual stocks.

Another advantage of index investing is its transparency. Because index funds and ETFs are designed to track specific market indexes, investors can easily see the underlying holdings of the fund and make informed decisions about their investments.

However, it is important to note that index investing is not without its limitations. While index funds and ETFs are designed to track specific market indexes, they may not perfectly replicate the performance of the underlying index due to factors such as tracking error and fees. Additionally, because index investing is a passive strategy, it may not provide the potential for outsized returns that can come with active management.

Overall, index investing can be a simple and effective way for investors to achieve broad market exposure while minimizing costs and risks associated with active management. However, it is important for investors to understand the limitations of this strategy and to consider their individual goals and risk tolerance before making any investment decisions.

CHAPTER SIX

RETIREMENT PLANNING

Planning for retirement is an important aspect of investing, and it's never too early to start. In this section, we will cover everything you need to know about retirement planning, including understanding the different retirement accounts, calculating retirement savings needs, and creating a retirement income plan. Whether you're just starting your career or nearing retirement age, this section will provide you with valuable information and strategies to help you plan for a comfortable and financially secure retirement.

Overview of retirement accounts (401k, IRA, Roth IRA, etc.)

Saving for retirement is one of the most important financial goals that many people have. To help people achieve this goal, there are several types of retirement accounts available in the United States and other countries, each with its own rules, tax benefits, and limitations. Here is an overview of the most common types of retirement accounts:

401(k) Plans: A 401(k) is a retirement savings plan sponsored by an employer. Employees can contribute a portion of their paycheck to the plan before taxes are taken out, reducing their taxable income. The money in the 401(k) grows tax-free until it is withdrawn at retirement. Some employers offer matching contributions, which can significantly boost retirement savings.

Traditional IRAs: An Individual Retirement Account (IRA) is a retirement savings account that individuals can open on their own. Like a 401(k), contributions to a traditional IRA are made pre-tax, reducing taxable income. Up to the time of withdrawal in retirement, the money grows tax-free. However, there are annual contribution limits, and withdrawals before age 59 1/2 may be subject to a penalty.

Roth IRAs: A Roth IRA is another type of retirement savings account that individuals can open on their own.

Unlike traditional IRAs, contributions to a Roth IRA are made after-tax, meaning they are not tax-deductible. However, the money in a Roth IRA grows tax-free and qualified withdrawals are tax-free in retirement. Roth IRAs also have annual contribution limits and restrictions based on income.

SEP IRAs: Simplified Employee Pension (SEP) IRAs are retirement plans that employers can set up for their employees. Employers make contributions to the plan on behalf of their employees. SEP IRAs have higher contribution limits than traditional and Roth IRAs, making them a good option for self-employed individuals or small business owners.

Solo 401(k) Plans: A Solo 401(k) is a retirement savings plan designed for self-employed individuals or small business owners without employees (other than a spouse). It works similarly to a traditional 401(k), allowing pre-tax contributions and offering the potential for employer contributions. Solo 401(k)s offer higher contribution limits than traditional or Roth IRAs, making them a good option for those with higher incomes.

Overall, understanding the different types of retirement accounts and their benefits and limitations is crucial when planning for retirement. Each type of account has its own unique features, so it's important to evaluate them based on individual financial goals and circumstances.

How to choose the right retirement account

When it comes to planning for retirement, choosing the right retirement account is crucial. The right account can help you maximize your savings and minimize your taxes, while the wrong account can leave you with fewer savings and a bigger tax bill. Here are some factors to consider when choosing the right retirement account for you:

Tax benefits: One of the main reasons to use a retirement account is for the tax benefits. Traditional 401(k) and IRA accounts allow you to contribute pre-tax dollars, which reduces your taxable income in the year of contribution.

This means you'll pay less in taxes each year, and your investments can grow tax-free until you withdraw them in retirement. Roth 401(k) and IRA accounts, on the other hand, are funded with after-tax dollars, but your investments can grow tax-free and qualified withdrawals in retirement are tax-free.

Employer contributions: If your employer offers a retirement plan, such as a 401(k), be sure to take advantage of any employer contributions. Many employers offer a matching contribution, where they will match a portion of your contributions up to a certain percentage of your salary. This is essentially free money, so it's important to take advantage of it if it's available.

Investment options: Some retirement accounts offer more investment options than others. For example, a self-directed IRA allows you to invest in a wider range of assets, including individual stocks and real estate. A 401(k) may only offer a limited number of mutual funds or target-date funds. Consider your investment preferences and the available options when choosing a retirement account.

Fees: Fees can eat into your investment returns, so it's important to consider the fees associated with different retirement accounts. Some accounts may have higher administrative fees or investment fees than others, so be sure to compare the costs of different options.

Contribution limits: Each retirement account has different contribution limits, which may change from year to year. Be sure to understand the contribution limits of the account you choose, as well as any catch-up contributions that may be available if you're over age 50.

Withdrawal rules: Finally, consider the withdrawal rules for the retirement account. Traditional 401(k) and IRA accounts require you to begin taking required minimum distributions (RMDs) at age 72, while Roth accounts do not have RMDs. There may also be penalties for withdrawing funds before age 59 ½, so be sure to understand the withdrawal rules before choosing a retirement account.

Ultimately, the right retirement account for you will depend on your individual circumstances and preferences. Consider working with a financial advisor to determine the best retirement savings strategy for your goals and needs.

Investing for retirement

Investing for retirement is an important consideration for many people. As you approach retirement age, it's important to ensure that you have enough money saved up to live comfortably during your retirement years. There are a few key things to keep in mind when investing for retirement.

Start early: The sooner you begin to save for retirement, the better. By starting early, you have more time to take advantage of compound interest, which can help your retirement savings grow significantly over time. It's never too late to begin saving for retirement, regardless of how late you're starting.

Set a goal: Before you start investing for retirement, it's important to have a clear idea of what your retirement goals are. This includes determining how much money you'll need to save in order to maintain your desired lifestyle during retirement. Consider factors like where you want to live, what activities you want to pursue, and any potential healthcare costs you may incur.

Determine your risk tolerance: When investing for retirement, it's important to consider your risk tolerance. This refers to your ability and willingness to handle fluctuations in the value of your investments. Generally, younger investors may be more willing to take on risk in order to achieve higher returns, while older investors may want to focus on more conservative investments to preserve their savings.

Diversify your portfolio: A key principle of investing for retirement is diversification. This means investing in a variety of asset classes, such as stocks, bonds, and real estate, to help spread out risk and potentially increase returns. In addition to reducing market volatility, diversification helps shield your portfolio.

Take advantage of tax-advantaged accounts: There are a number of tax-advantaged retirement accounts available, such as 401(k)s, IRAs, and Roth IRAs. These accounts allow you to invest for retirement while enjoying certain tax benefits, such as tax-deferred growth or tax-free withdrawals in retirement.

Consider working with a financial advisor: Investing for retirement can be complex, and it can be helpful to work with a financial advisor who can help you navigate the various options available to you. A financial advisor can help you create a personalized retirement plan based on your goals and risk tolerance, and can provide guidance on investment selection, portfolio diversification, and other important considerations.

Overall, investing for retirement requires careful consideration and planning. By starting early, setting clear goals, diversifying your portfolio, and taking advantage of tax-advantaged accounts, you can help ensure that you have enough money saved up to enjoy a comfortable retirement.

Withdrawal strategies

Withdrawal strategies refer to the methods used to access funds from retirement accounts during retirement. It is important to have a plan in place for withdrawing funds to ensure that they last throughout retirement. There are several withdrawal strategies that retirees can use to manage their retirement income.

One common withdrawal strategy is the systematic withdrawal approach, which involves withdrawing a fixed percentage of the account balance each year. For example, if the retiree has $500,000 in retirement savings and decides to withdraw 4% per year, they would receive $20,000 per year in retirement income. This strategy is known as the 4% rule and has been widely studied and debated among financial professionals.

Another approach is the bucket strategy, which involves dividing retirement savings into different buckets based on the time horizon for each bucket. For example, a retiree might put money into short-term, mid-term, and long-term buckets. The short-term bucket might be for immediate expenses, such as living expenses for the next one to three years. The mid-term bucket might be for expenses that are three to ten years away, such as a new car or home repairs. The long-term bucket might be for expenses that are more than ten years away, such as a grandchild's college education or a dream vacation. This approach allows retirees to manage their expenses based on their time horizon.

Another withdrawal strategy is to use a guaranteed income source, such as an annuity. An annuity is a contract between the retiree and an insurance company that provides a guaranteed income stream for life or for a set period of time. Annuities can provide a steady source of income and can help retirees manage the risk of outliving their savings.

Retirees can also use a combination of these strategies to manage their retirement income. For example, they might use the 4% rule for immediate expenses, the bucket strategy for mid-term expenses, and an annuity for long-term expenses.

It is important for retirees to keep in mind that withdrawal strategies are not set in stone and may need to be adjusted over time based on changes in their financial situation or market conditions. Retirees should also be aware of any tax implications of their withdrawal strategy and work with a financial advisor to ensure they are making the most informed decisions for their retirement income.

CHAPTER SEVEN

TIPS FOR SUCCESSFUL INVESTING

Investing can be a daunting task, but with the right strategies and mindset, it can also be a rewarding one. In this section, we will discuss some tips for successful investing. These tips will help you navigate the market with confidence and make informed decisions about your investments. We will cover topics such as staying disciplined, avoiding emotional decisions, setting realistic expectations, diversifying your portfolio, and monitoring your investments regularly. By following these tips, you can increase your chances of achieving your financial goals and building long-term wealth.

Importance of a long-term outlook

Investing is all about achieving long-term financial goals. Whether you're investing for retirement, building wealth, or saving for a major life event, it's important to have a long-term outlook when making investment decisions. This means looking beyond short-term market fluctuations and focusing on the bigger picture.

One of the biggest mistakes investors make is trying to time the market or chase quick gains. Market timing involves trying to predict the future direction of the market and buying or selling assets accordingly. This is a risky strategy, as even experienced investors often get it wrong. Trying to chase quick gains can also be detrimental, as it often involves taking on too much risk in the hopes of making a big profit in a short period of time. This type of investing is more akin to gambling than true investing.

Instead of trying to time the market or chase quick gains, successful investors focus on long-term trends and fundamentals. They understand that markets go up and down, but over the long-term, they tend to rise. By taking a long-term approach, investors can avoid the emotional rollercoaster of short-term market volatility and make more informed investment decisions based on the underlying value of the assets they're buying.

Another benefit of a long-term outlook is that it allows investors to take advantage of compound interest. The idea of generating interest on interest is known as compound interest. For example, if you invest $10,000 in a stock that has an average annual return of 8%, after one year, your investment will be worth $10,800. If you leave that money invested for another year, it will earn interest on the full $10,800, not just the original $10,000. This compounding effect has the potential to significantly increase the value of your investment portfolio over time.

In addition to the benefits of compound interest, taking a long-term approach also allows investors to benefit from the power of diversification. By spreading your investments across different asset classes and sectors, you can reduce your overall risk and increase your chances of achieving long-term financial goals. Diversification can also help smooth out short-term market fluctuations, as losses in one area of your portfolio may be offset by gains in another.

Ultimately, investing with a long-term outlook requires patience, discipline, and a commitment to your financial goals. By avoiding the temptation to chase quick gains and focusing on long-term trends and fundamentals, investors can build a solid investment portfolio that can help them achieve their financial objectives over time.

Staying disciplined and avoiding emotional decisions

Staying disciplined and avoiding emotional decisions is crucial for successful investing. As humans, we often fall prey to cognitive biases and emotions that can cloud our judgment and lead to irrational decisions. This can result in buying high and selling low, chasing after the latest investment trend, or panicking during a market downturn and selling off investments.

One of the most common emotional biases that investors face is the fear of missing out, or FOMO. This can lead to investors jumping into hot stocks or sectors without conducting proper due diligence or having a solid investment strategy. The result can be costly mistakes and significant losses.

Another common emotional bias is loss aversion, where investors are more sensitive to losses than gains. This can lead investors to hold onto losing investments for too long, hoping they will recover, or selling winning investments too early to lock in gains, missing out on potential future growth.

To avoid these emotional biases, investors should develop a sound investment plan and stick to it. This plan should be based on their financial goals, risk tolerance, and time horizon. Investors should also conduct proper due diligence before making any investment decisions, such as researching the company, industry, or market trends, and analysing the investment's financial performance and risks.

Additionally, investors should diversify their portfolio to reduce risk and volatility. By investing in a mix of different asset classes, such as stocks, bonds, and real estate, investors can spread their risk across different sectors and industries, and mitigate the effect of any investment's bad performance on their portfolio as a whole.

Staying disciplined also means avoiding impulsive decisions during times of market volatility or uncertainty. It can be tempting to sell off investments during a market downturn, but this can result in significant losses and missed opportunities when the market eventually recovers. Instead, investors should stay focused on their long-term goals and stick to their investment plan.

It is also essential to avoid the temptation to constantly monitor investment performance and make changes based on short-term fluctuations. Checking account balances daily or weekly can lead to unnecessary anxiety and emotional decision-making. Instead, investors should review their portfolio periodically, such as annually or semi-annually, to ensure it is aligned with their long-term investment objectives.

Lastly, working with a financial advisor can help investors stay disciplined and avoid emotional decisions. A qualified financial advisor can provide guidance and objective advice on investment decisions, help develop a personalized investment plan, and keep investors accountable to their long-term goals.

In summary, staying disciplined and avoiding emotional decisions is essential for successful investing. By developing a sound investment plan, conducting proper due diligence, diversifying their portfolio, and staying focused on their long-term goals, investors can make informed decisions that align with their financial objectives. Working with a financial advisor can also provide valuable guidance and accountability to help investors stay disciplined and avoid making costly emotional decisions.

Staying informed and keeping up with the market

Investing in the stock market is an excellent way to grow your wealth over the long term, but it requires a disciplined approach and a willingness to stay informed about the latest developments in the market. Staying informed and keeping up with the market can help you make informed decisions and avoid costly mistakes.

One of the most important ways to stay informed about the stock market is to read financial news and analysis regularly. Financial news outlets such as CNBC, Bloomberg, and The Wall Street Journal provide daily updates on the stock market, including the latest trends, market movements, and analysis of individual stocks and sectors. You can also find valuable insights from financial blogs, podcasts, and newsletters.

It's also important to stay up to date on the companies and sectors you're interested in investing in. This means keeping track of their financial performance, including earnings reports, revenue growth, and key financial metrics. You can find this information on financial websites such as Yahoo Finance, Google Finance, and MarketWatch, as well as on the websites of individual companies.

Another important way to stay informed about the stock market is to follow the advice of expert investors and analysts. Many successful investors share their insights and strategies through books, blogs, podcasts, and interviews. By learning from these experts, you can gain valuable insights into the stock market and improve your investment performance.

In addition to staying informed, it's also important to stay disciplined and avoid emotional decisions when investing in the stock market. This means sticking to your investment strategy, even when the market experiences short-term fluctuations or downturns. It can be tempting to make impulsive decisions when the market is volatile, but this often leads to poor investment performance.

One way to stay disciplined is to set clear investment goals and develop a long-term investment strategy. This should include an asset allocation plan that balances risk and return, as well as a diversification strategy that spreads your investments across different asset classes, sectors, and geographies.

Another way to stay disciplined is to avoid trying to time the market or chase short-term trends. Instead, focus on investing for the long term and taking advantage of the power of compounding to grow your wealth over time.

Finally, it's important to avoid common investment pitfalls such as overconfidence, herd mentality, and confirmation bias. Overconfidence can lead investors to take on too much risk or make overly aggressive investments, while herd mentality can lead investors to follow the crowd and make the same investment decisions as everyone else, regardless of their own financial goals and risk tolerance. Confirmation bias can cause investors to seek out information that confirms their existing beliefs, rather than objectively evaluating all available information.

In summary, staying informed and keeping up with the market is essential for successful investing. This means reading financial news and analysis regularly, staying up to date on the companies and sectors you're interested in, and following the advice of expert investors and analysts. It also means staying disciplined and avoiding emotional decisions, sticking to your investment strategy, and avoiding common investment pitfalls. By following these principles, you can improve your investment performance and achieve your financial goals over the long term.

Importance of diversification

Diversification is a key component of any successful investment strategy. The basic idea behind diversification is to spread your investments across multiple asset classes, industries, and geographic regions, in order to reduce risk and increase the chances of long-term growth. By diversifying your investments, you are less exposed to the risks associated with any one company or sector, and more likely to capture the returns of the broader market.

One of the primary benefits of diversification is that it can help reduce volatility in your portfolio. When you invest in just one or a few individual stocks or bonds, your portfolio is subject to the ups and downs of those particular assets. If one of those assets experiences a sharp decline, it can have a significant impact on your overall portfolio value. By diversifying your holdings, you can help cushion the impact of any one asset's decline.

Another benefit of diversification is the potential for higher long-term returns. While diversification may reduce the potential for outsized gains from a single investment, it also reduces the potential for outsized losses. By spreading your investments across a broad range of assets, you increase the likelihood of capturing the long-term growth potential of the overall market. This can lead to more consistent and predictable returns over time.

There are many ways to achieve diversification in your investment portfolio. One of the most common is through the use of mutual funds and exchange-traded funds (ETFs). These investment vehicles provide exposure to a broad range of stocks, bonds, and other assets, and can be a convenient and cost-effective way to achieve diversification. Many mutual funds and ETFs are designed to track specific indexes, such as the S&P 500 or the Dow Jones Industrial Average, providing investors with exposure to the broader market.

Another way to achieve diversification is through asset allocation. You do this by distributing your portfolio among various asset types, including stocks, bonds, and cash. The idea behind asset allocation is to balance risk and return by investing in a mix of assets that are appropriate for your investment goals, time horizon, and risk tolerance.

It's also important to consider geographic diversification when investing. This involves investing in assets from different regions of the world, such as Europe, Asia, and emerging markets. By investing in assets from different regions, you can reduce the impact of any one region's economic or political instability on your portfolio.

While diversification is an important component of any investment strategy, it's important to keep in mind that it does not eliminate risk entirely. All investments carry some degree of risk, and diversification cannot protect against all types of risk, such as market risk, inflation risk, or currency risk. However, by diversifying your investments across multiple asset classes, industries, and geographic regions, you can help reduce your exposure to specific types of risk and increase your chances of long-term success.

In order to achieve the benefits of diversification, it's important to have a clear understanding of your investment goals, risk tolerance, and time horizon. This can help you determine the appropriate asset allocation and diversification strategy for your portfolio. Additionally, it's important to periodically review and rebalance your portfolio to ensure that it remains aligned with your investment goals and risk tolerance. Regularly rebalancing your portfolio can also help ensure that you continue to capture the benefits of diversification over time.

CHAPTER EIGHT

CONCLUSION

As you have read through this guide, you have gained a solid understanding of the key principles and strategies of successful investing. You have learned about the importance of setting clear investment goals, assessing your risk tolerance, creating a budget, building an emergency fund, and selecting the right mix of investments for your portfolio. You have also explored different investment strategies and retirement accounts, as well as tips for successful long-term investing. By putting these concepts into practice, you can achieve financial security and grow your wealth over time. Remember, successful investing requires patience, discipline, and a commitment to ongoing learning and improvement. With the knowledge you have gained, you are well on your way to building a strong foundation for your financial future.

Recap of key points

Smart Investing Made Easy: A Beginner's Guide to Building a Portfolio has covered a lot of ground when it comes to investing. As a beginner, it can be overwhelming to learn everything at once, but by breaking down the concepts into digestible sections, this guide has made it easier for readers to understand the basics of investing.

One of the key takeaways from this guide is the importance of setting investment goals. Whether it's saving for retirement, building wealth, or achieving financial freedom, having a clear goal in mind can help guide your investment decisions.

Another important factor in successful investing is assessing your risk tolerance. Understanding how much risk you're comfortable with and how it relates to potential returns is crucial when deciding on asset allocation and diversification.

Building a budget and creating an emergency fund are two foundational steps to take before investing. By having a solid financial foundation, you can better weather any unexpected financial setbacks that may arise.

When it comes to building a portfolio, asset allocation and diversification are key concepts to understand. By spreading your investments across different asset classes, you can minimize risk and potentially increase returns.

Within your portfolio, choosing individual stocks and bonds, investing in mutual funds and ETFs, and index investing are all strategies to consider. It's important to remember the importance of low fees, as they can eat away at your returns over time.

When it comes to investment strategies, value investing, growth investing, and income investing are all viable options depending on your investment goals and risk tolerance.

Retirement planning is an important aspect of investing, and there are various retirement accounts to consider, including 401k, IRA, and Roth IRA. Choosing the right retirement account depends on your individual circumstances and goals.

Staying disciplined, avoiding emotional decisions, and staying informed are all important factors in successful investing. Additionally, maintaining a long-term outlook and practicing diversification can help you weather market fluctuations and achieve your investment goals.

Overall, Smart Investing Made Easy: A Beginner's Guide to Building a Portfolio provides a comprehensive overview of the fundamentals of investing. By understanding these key concepts, beginners can feel more confident in making informed investment decisions and working towards achieving their financial goals.

Final thoughts and encouragement for readers to start investing

Congratulations! You have made it to the end of this beginner's guide to investing. By now, you should have a good understanding of the different types of investments, the importance of asset allocation, diversification, and fees, and the various investment strategies that can help you achieve your financial goals. Investing can seem intimidating, but it is a crucial step in securing your financial future, and the earlier you start, the better.

If you have not started investing yet, it is never too late to begin. It is important to remember that investing is a long-term commitment, and success is not achieved overnight. It takes patience, discipline, and a willingness to learn from mistakes. Here are some final thoughts and encouragement for those who are ready to take the plunge into investing:

Start small and gradually increase your investments: You do not have to start with a large sum of money. In fact, it is often recommended to start small and gradually increase your investments as you become more comfortable with the process. Starting small also allows you to learn from any mistakes you may make without risking a significant amount of money.

Do your research: Before making any investment, it is important to research the company, mutual fund, or ETF you plan to invest in. Look for their financial statements, earnings reports, and any news articles related to the company. Doing your research will give you a better understanding of the investment and help you make informed decisions.

Stay disciplined: One of the most important things you can do as an investor is to stay disciplined. This entails sticking to your investment strategy and refraining from making snap judgments based on momentary market swings. It can be tempting to sell your investments during a market downturn, but staying disciplined and staying invested can lead to long-term success.

Don't be afraid to ask for help: Investing can be complex, and it is okay to seek help from a financial advisor or a trusted friend or family member who has experience investing. They can help you navigate the investment landscape and provide guidance on investment strategies that align with your goals.

Remember your long-term goals: When investing, it is important to keep your long-term goals in mind. Whether it is saving for retirement, buying a home, or paying for your children's education, having a clear understanding of your goals can help you make better investment decisions.

In conclusion, investing is an important part of securing your financial future, and it is never too early or too late to start. By following the tips and advice in this guide, you can make informed investment decisions, stay disciplined, and work towards achieving your financial goals. Remember, investing is a long-term commitment, and success is achieved through patience, discipline, and a willingness to learn from mistakes. Good luck on your investing journey!